BIG TRUCKS

NEW SEASONS
PUBLISHING

Copyright © 1990 Publications International, Ltd.
ISBN 0-88176-848-0
Illustrated by: Mike Muir

Tractor trailer trucks are really big. This one is loaded with toys. The other truck is delivering barrels of pickles. All sorts of things are brought to stores by tractor trailer trucks.

Car carriers deliver new cars all over the country. These cars were loaded on this car carrier at the factory. The ramps will go down, and workers will drive the new cars off the truck. Maybe this car carrier will deliver your new car.

Moving vans are so exciting. When someone moves, a moving van parks in front of their old house and the movers put all their furniture in the moving van. Then they drive to their new house where they will unpack their things. When a moving van stops on your street, it means new neighbors and maybe a new friend.

Dump trucks are so big. They haul away dirt and rocks. A cement mixer is big, too. Its huge drum goes round and round getting the cement ready to pour. Maybe this one will pour a new street or sidewalk.

Flashing lights and a loud siren tell cars and other trucks to make way for the fire truck. It also has ladders to reach tall buildings and big hoses to spray water on fires. See how quickly they put the fire out.

Lumber trucks carry wood from the forest to the lumber mill. A big saw will cut the logs into boards. These boards could be used for houses, furniture, or even wooden toys.

Cars need gasoline to make them go. Tanker trucks deliver gasoline to gas stations where it is poured into big underground tanks. When your car needs gas, you drive it to the pump and fill it up!

Here comes the garbage truck rumbling down your street. A garbage collector throws all of your garbage into the back of the truck where it is crunched. This way there is room for your neighbors' garbage in the truck, too.